Bollocks to

Bollocks to Brexit

an Anthology of Poems and Short Fiction

Edited by Ambrose Musiyiwa

Civic ♥ Leicester

First published in Great Britain in 2019 by
CivicLeicester

Civic ♥ Leicester

y. https://www.youtube.com/user/CivicLeicester

f. https://www.facebook.com/CivicLeicester

CivicLeicester@gmail.com

ISBN-13: 978-1-9164593-3-5

Dedicated to the one who knew they could fly
and wasn't afraid of falling

CONTENTS

Bollocks to Brexit:
an Anthology of Poems and Short Fiction

PREFACE

THE POETRY OF the Twentieth Century's two world wars can easily be seen as the vanguard of contemporary protest poetry in its nakedly political subject matter and refusal to allow politicians and the officer class to dodge their collective accountability. W. B Yeats may have felt that "it is better in times like these / A poet's mouth be silent, for in truth / We have no gift to set a statesman right" but an entire corpus of poets, among them, Siegfried Sassoon and Wilfred Owen, who didn't have the option of fence-sitting, disagreed.

Granted, radical British poetry stretches back much further – Shelley's 'The Masque of Anarchy' (1819) remains a rousing call to action, while Robert Burns baited the establishment in poem after poem – but the shattering human cost of global conflict was on a scale hitherto unimaginable. Poetry did not remain silent. Poetry responded.

Post-World War II, change came quickly – social, political, economic and artistic change. Britain tried to cling on to its faded Edwardian principles during the 1950s, but it couldn't last. The "angry young man" movement saw to that. Working class writers suddenly had a platform.

The 1960s opened the floodgates: youth found its voice; students became politically active. Mass CND protests were held against nuclear armaments. Students on both sides of the Atlantic condemned US military presence in Indochina. A generation of poets and activists took Adrian Mitchell's 'Tell Me Lies About Vietnam' as their anthem.

As the passion and idealism of the 1960s segued into the cynicism of the 1970s, a decade of turmoil that itself segued into the 1980s' repellent doctrine of Thatcherism, poetry continued to respond. Ken Smith and Tony Harrison wrote hard-hitting dispatches from a Britain scarred by worsening social division. Harrison's book-length poem 'V' remains chilling and relevant today.

More recently poetry has flourished on the internet, with online journals like The Stare's Nest, Poetry24 and I Am Not A Silent Poet providing a platform for response poems, protest poems and the literature of resistance. Independent publishers continue to fly the flag for socialist and radical writers: Shoestring Press, Five Leaves, Smokestack Press, Burning Eye Books, Culture Matters – so many in fact that it's a salutary reminder of how much there still is to protest against.

The title of this anthology makes its protest clear. Brexit is the great lie of our generation. The Leave campaign was based on false promises, blatant lies and a rhetoric of nostalgia for a Britain that never was. Latent xenophobia came to the surface. Far-right hate groups like Britain First and the EDL hijacked social media, using mainstream tactics to push a racist agenda. Facebook's recent ban of both groups is welcome but far too late.

The Brexit fallout is, at time of writing, a weird blend of farce and disaster. We have a grossly incompetent Prime Minister clinging onto power even as her authority crumbles; an opposition party who could rally millions by opposing Brexit but don't; a breakaway "Independent" group whose members' self-interest does Remain no favours. We have no idea when Brexit will be delivered, in what form, and how debilitating the cost. Billions have already been squandered while a desperately under-resourced NHS flounders.

Most bizarrely of all, debate around Brexit seems shackled by the mindset, repeated *ad nauseum* by Parliament and press alike, that a second referendum would destroy the public's trust in the political process and cause division. This anthology has news for the establishment: our so-called leaders have lost the trust of the people; and this country is divided already.

And poetry responds. As it always has.

Neil Fulwood

Nottingham, April 2019

INTRODUCTION

IT IS 100 years since a peaceful gathering for parliamentary reform was brought to a violent end by the Manchester Yeomanry. Around a dozen people were killed and hundreds more injured in the Peterloo massacre. In response, Percy Shelley wrote 'The Masque of Anarchy', which was banned for 30 years.

In the late twentieth century, Peterloo Poets, an independent publisher which ran for 37 years until its founder's death in 2009, was established to honour the demonstrators who were caught up in that massacre.

Two years ago, a vast crowd gathered outside the town hall after the Manchester bombing, where they were addressed by the poet Tony Walsh, who referred to the city's suffragette past and who saluted the city's inclusive culture at a time which could otherwise have easily been divisive ("some were born here / some were drawn here"). Tony Walsh could also have been joined by other poets who had similarly saluted the city's history of political resistance without glossing over its unsavoury aspects, like its slavery past.

Peter Kalu's poem 'Manchester' speaks of slave barons as well as suffragettes and revolutionaries. Kalu has expressed his commitment to the need for poets to "bear witness to the times" by "documenting" events at home and abroad.

The Midlands has its own "alternative newscasters", to borrow the words of Benjamin Zephaniah, poets who remember the 1980s as a period of intense struggle against racism, a struggle which has re-emerged with Brexit. As the comedian Hardeep Singh Kohli points out, Brexit has resurfaced old racisms which are embedded within the psyche of a nation that still struggles to release itself from the grip of empire.

One month after Tony Walsh read his poem outside Manchester town hall, Grenfell Tower burned down in an avoidable disaster, predicted by the Grenfell Tower Action Group. Ben Okri writes, "I could not get that burning tower out of my head. Bearing witness seemed the only thing to do."

He describes seeing photographs of people marked as missing, staring out from posters that were pasted on the walls. "Then", he writes, "someone in the crowd was stabbing at the air with an accusing finger. I looked up and saw the spire of the church and, beyond it, like a spectre, like a biblical abomination, I saw the tower... like an evil omen... the tower of the dead, a vertical crematorium."

He wrote a poem for Grenfell. He wrote "if the people of Grenfell Tower had strong defenders in the corridors of power, then a fire in one of the rooms could never have had so catastrophic an effect. They had perished that way because they were poor."

To Okri, "political poetry has its source in the common river of humanity." It shows compassion, it analyses, it guides and it leads.

In Manchester, Tony Walsh urged his city to "choose love". In London, Okri decided it was his duty to craft a poem, because the poet needs to speak for more people than the individual poet alone. He wanted to stir the world to feel a common sense of outrage.

A video of his poem was viewed 6 million times.

Okri was by no means the first London-dweller to commemorate tragic and avoidable deaths in a fire: Linton Kwesi Johnson wrote 'New Cross Massahkah' to remember the deaths of 14 young black Britons in New Cross Road after an arson attack. Kwesi Johnson is included in Okri's edited anthology, *Rise Like Lions* (2018), a collection of political poems in multiple forms, from polemic to lyric. The collection also includes Shelley's banned poem 'The Masque of Anarchy'.

Leicester has its own traditions of political poetry, notably the work of Susanna Watts and Elizabeth Heyrick, who composed feminist poetry and organised a sugar boycott of slave-produced sugar in 1824.

Now, in 2019, Brexit has brought us trouble. It's time for poets to step into the breach. And, with *Bollocks to Brexit*, they have.

Dr Corinne Fowler
Leicester, May 2019

"BOLLOCKS" AND ITS USES: A SHORT HISTORY

THE VERY WORD "bollocks" and its use was dealt with back in 1977 when a shop manager was caught displaying the Sex Pistols' album, 'Never Mind the Bollocks' in the shop window.

The Court case went into detail about the word "bollocks". The barrister, John Mortimer, who was defending the shop manager called in an expert (yes I know we have all had enough of experts) witness, James Kinsley, who was a professor of English and also an Anglican priest.

He explained that the word "bollocks" has been around since Anglo-Saxon times to simply mean "a ball", it then became a nickname for a clergyman. Clergymen were known for talking a load of rubbish (just like... a lot like Brexiters do) so the word "bollocks" later developed to mean "nonsense".

John Mortimer asked the Court: 'What sort of country are we living in if a politician comes to Nottingham and speaks here to a group of people in the city centre and during his speech a heckler replies "Bollocks!". Are we to expect this person to be incarcerated, or do we live in a country where we are proud of our Anglo-Saxon language? Do we wish our language to be virile and strong or watered down and weak?'

John Mortimer elaborated on the use of the word "bollocks" explaining how in biblical texts 'it was used to describe small things of an appropriate shape.'

Further to this, 'the word also appears in place names without stirring any sensual desires in the local communities.' And our prime minister, Theresa May herself may be amused to read that, 'Mortimer mischievously suggested this would be similar to a city being called 'Maidenhead' which didn't seem to cause the locals… any problems.'

The magistrates after deliberation dismissed the case. The word "bollocks" on the album was not obscene.

Remember, all this bollocks already took place in 1977 and now it's taking place again in the 2010s!

Ofcom in 2016 produced a report – 'Attitudes to potentially offensive language and gestures on TV and radio' which detailed "bollocks" as follows:

'Medium language, potentially unacceptable pre-watershed. Not generally offensive but somewhat vulgar when used to refer to testicles. Less problematic when used to mean "nonsense"'.

Brexit *is* a load of nonsense. There is literally NO SENSE to Brexit and in this context it is quite clear and apparent that our use of the word "bollocks" is entirely appropriate. "NONSENSE TO BREXIT!" doesn't exactly have the same kind of ring to it – does it?

Joel Baccas
London, April 2019

The Questions of Our Children

The danger of nostalgia:
dragging our children into a future,
where they will look back
and ask why this happened.

Ask why we acted,
With no sense and no plan,
and demand an explanation.
Because they *will* demand an explanation.

Will we tell them we were fed
on impossible promises?
Or explain it as a hunger
for supposed 'past glories'?

Gluttonous and ignorant,
we saw we were wrong.
But, too stubborn to back down,
we dragged ourselves along.

Our children will understand
they have to do better
to prevent their own kids
from suffering at their hands
and turning to them, broken,
to demand an explanation.

Jacob Spivey

I believe in EU

So farewell then to Europe, it's sad we have to leave.
Please don't think too bad of us, there are still many who believe,
that EU made us thrive, share a common aim,
speak with strength on a global stage, and not go to war again.

But bigoted nostalgists would set us back
to darker times when fascists came to power.
"We must respect the people's voice!", we hear the PM claim,
[aside] "But now they know the awful truth; we won't ask *them* again!"

So as we, with trepidation, stumble forward with blinkered sight,
following unicorn dreams of greatness (in truth little more than shite),
I want to look the leavers in the face and with all my power scream,
I MAY BE STUCK IN BRITAIN BUT I'M STILL A EUROPEAN!

Pappageno

Business as...

- What about all this Brexit stuff then?
- I didn't vote.
- They're all the same, aren't they?
- It'll be fine. We survived the second world war.
- Working?
- Nah, not at the minute. Lost my job at Dyson. They're moving abroad.
- Aye. We were at that food bank. Didn't realise it was that bad. I'll find something soon.
- Lost the house last week. Crept up on me. The wife's sister took her in. I'll be OK.
- It says in the paper the army is coming to help.

Danielle Allen

When We Weren't Looking

When we weren't looking
Too busy with our digits
On our mobile phones
They came and stole our souls
Not all at once
Or we might have noticed
But bit by bit
Until one day
We were unable to see
The Unicorns grazing
In the pastures
Of our minds.

When we weren't looking
They came and stole our words
One by one
They disappeared
And we did not argue
But watched
As the poetry died.

When we weren't looking
They came and stole imagination
So we could no longer dream
Aspire or strive.

When we weren't looking
They came and stole all hope
And to our shame
We just acquiesced.

Trefor Stockwell

Peregrines
peregrine (*adjective*) – *coming from another country.*

We thought it was the catch of breath that forecasts heavy weather:
something fretful in the leaves, the weathercocks in a spin.

When nightingales called *cheer-up*, *jug-jug*, the grouse replied *go-back*;
the hedgerows emptied quickly, in a gale of fleeing wings.

In the spring, a leaflet fluttered through each letterbox:
Even the blackbirds in your garden came from Eastern Europe.

Brent geese wheeled north, oaring the air for Svalbard;
fieldfares left their seafaring, turned tail for the fjords.

The whole sky dark with them – a rain of down and droppings.
A year with a silent summer, and our islands cast adrift.

My grandmother's ashes stirred beneath a Sussex apple tree,
restless for the crossing home to Chemin des Fauconniers.

I could only name my estrangement in words with distant origins,
and all that was peregrine in me quivered to take flight.

Yvonne Reddick

To the tune of 350 million pounds

The lies on the bus go round-and-round
Round-and-round
Round-and-round
The lies on the bus go round-and-round
All campaign long
Gaffes on the bus go round-and-round
Round-and-round
Round-and-round
Gaffes on the bus go round-and-round
All BoJo long
Weasel on the bus go round-and-round
Round-and-round
Round-and-round
Weasel on the bus go round-and-round
All the Gove long
Sneers on the bus go round-and-round
Round-and-round
Round-and-round
Sneers on the bus go round-and-round
All IDS long
The NHS on the bus no round-and-round
No round-and-round
No round-and-round
The NHS on the bus no round-and-round
Brexit tried to kill it

Anthony L. Church

Brexit Exit
(a dance performance in the DMU Gallery, which coincidentally housed a
collection of pictures of derelict factories)

She talks of the loss of openness,
this Portuguese dancer who is leaving;
she dances surrounded by large photos of openness,
open spaces where our factories used to be.
Huge flat concrete open spaces,
with a few derelict chimneys sticking up pointlessly,
subject to preservation orders.

It's now a bullshit artist's Britain,
where you can't knock down old chimneys,
but can't put smoke up them either;
where nothing much is made anymore.
These are the fruits of openness:
these devastated landscapes,
the blighted future of those who used to work in them.

She is leaving because of Brexit, this Portuguese,
but – she is leaving at the right time;
even had there been no Brexit.

Stephen Wylie

after years of putting her down john bull kicks europa out of his house and embraces a bright new future where he makes his own rules.

Monday.
and John shrugs his shoulders
says it's been coming for a while
plenty more fish out there, you know
another lager, landlord! smiles
slides money over the bar
breathes deep and crows of freedom
sinks the pint, again again again.

Tuesday.
he's back down the pub
telling anyone who's there
that he's fine without her
no more gip about leaving
the toilet seat up
no earache when he has
a harmless daytime tipple
he's living the dream, people!
you saps should try it.

Wednesday.
she needs him more than he needs her
you'll see, she'll be back, the bitch,
mark his words
crawling on her fucking knees.

Thursday.
pissed, he mutters about betrayal
shoots dark glances round the bar
asks for the loan of a tenner
till, well... whenever
you learn who your friends are
someone helped her take the bloody sofa
yer bastards, you lot, bastards.

Friday.
she's been seen walking out
with another fella on her arm
looking good, someone says
before they're shushed to silence
and they all try to pretend
they can't hear the sound
of a proud man lost
and sobbing in the toilets.

Steve Pottinger

Marooned

Between the tears and snots
and the chill February fret,
the wailsong of regret
tolls heavy round the prom
in pidgin English.

Marooned on an island
she cries down the line
But this is not acceptable!
but the sob from her chest
has already accepted it.

Outside bolted doors,
these wintry shores
have seen much warmer times.

Harry Gallagher

Yes, there will also be singing
After Bertolt Brecht, motto to Svendborg Poems, 1939

When this nation broke with Rome
men left enough of the abbey standing
so sailors could still steer their ships
by its shattered walls.

We were less cautious.
We saw the darkness creeping in
heard our fog horns sound a warning
from the lighthouse on the cliff
but in our madness we cast off.

Up there somewhere
candles are burning
parishioners huddle around the stove.
They are singing the only poem
to survive.

Deborah Harvey

Whitby Abbey was ruined during the dissolution of the monasteries in 1540.

Cædmon, the earliest English poet whose name we know, was a monk at the Abbey in the 7th century. Only one of his poems has come down to us.

Toby's Singing

What a glorious feelin'
I'm happy again -
I'm laughing at clouds,
and I'm ready for love.

It is raining.
This is June 2016 and this is England,
we have voted to leave Europe.
Goodbye sweet continent
of happy food and happy sunshine
and bugger-like subjunctive clauses.

I'm ready for love, sings Toby,
I'm singing in the rain.
We're all singing in the rain
or rather we're not singing
in the rain, we're just standing
in the rain listening to Toby.

Seagulls clatter, swoop, hover,
or stand on the gazebo and they too
are singing – We're ready for love
and blah de blah de blah in the rain
'cos we're English seagulls
and we love the bleeding rain.

In Aldeburgh the tea rooms are full
of people eating scones
and being nostalgic about the Blitz.
Wasn't it marvellous, they say
the way we sang and carried on.

We pulled ourselves up by the bootstraps
and shoved an inordinate amount
of pork pie and skate wing down our throats.

Monica says, vis-à-vis the seagulls,
(Monica's writing a YA novel and comes
from Melbourne) They're drones!

I know you'll find that a bugger to believe
but I've done my research, tedious
amounts of it, and those sea gulls swooping
and swaying and going backwards and
shitting in the wind are bloody drones.

Julian Stannard

March

is the month of untruths
where the clock is winding down
to D-Day, decision time, the tide
of protests is swelling and the resignations
of old notions is drenching the air grey,

the rhythms of anger are beating
harder on the door of number ten
the tongues in the House
abuse and disabuse the word
democracy, until nobody knows

what it means anymore, it may
as well be an Arabic word
for chaos, we wouldn't know.
The carpets of the rich are getting
redder with the blood of the poor,

the lies of the last two and a half
years, are the toads being squashed
on both city and country roads.
It is time to march and give the month
new meaning. It is time to wind up

the clock and spring forward from
St. Melangell's cloak, time to roll up
the aisle of daffodils, who only know
the music of hope. It is time. It is
time. It is time.

Bethany Rivers

Uncertainties

Do you remember how much we laughed back then -
The Millennium still young, everyone confident
in the new century, its hopeful clarity?
And then this old American, Rumsfelt,
standing before a press conference
trying to explain government intelligence.
For weeks we played with his phrases:
the possibilities of the weekend were known unknowns,
the inevitability of Monday morning was a known known,
our unexpected breakdown on the M6
was an unknown unknown.
There was even talk of a publication:
the Collected Poetry of Donald Rumsfelt.

And now, as I try to work out how we got into this mess,
his words come flooding back to me.
I was so sure we'd want to Remain in Europe –
our jobs depended on it, our national security,
even the trivialities of our summer package holidays.
And yet, just days before the vote,
didn't our friends, campaigning on the streets,
warn us against complacency?
And that man we spoke to in the charity shop -
didn't he say surely we'd vote Out because, like him,
we'd want our Sovereignty back?

Did Cameron, in his arrogance, assume
the outcome was a certainty, a known known,
while around him worried advisers
shook their heads in disbelief?
Were the possibilities of negotiations
discussed in terms of known unknowns?
Did civil servants, even then, envisage
this headlong plunge over the cliff face,
this hurtle into unknown unknowns?

Angi Holden

War in a Time of Love

A nation now not of shopkeepers but of shoppers,
this small country of small minds, ancient monsters
rising from its media deeps, white-haired old ladies
who have not a second thought
on the committing of mass murder
saying, when interviewed in the street,
"We are an island State, of course,
we must protect ourselves." (During the Falklands fiasco
similar old ladies actually and unashamedly declared,
"Nuke Argentina.") Now the newer adherents of misprinted bibles
likewise condemn all their not-of-them; or they follow the porn god
who says, "Believe, this is what men and women want."
Troglodyte generations now in the dark of indoors,
heads inside their screens, playing x-box shoot-to-kill,
or jeering at politicians as they scrabble to keep up
with the consequences of their blatherings,
supported in their incidental
(deliberate?) fear-making
by the foreign-owned Sun and Daily Mail.
No pity in their pages for the mud-smeared wandering poor.
As for the rest of us - we're told at every turn,
by the stern-voiced enforcers of conformity, that
if we are of no use to them
then we are worthless.
So be it.

Sam Smith

Magical Thinking

On this sinking island, this listing ship—

let's wake up tomorrow and discover
that the referendum result was just a bad dream

and that Clinton was elected and she turned out okay
that Corbyn was elected in the end and he turned out okay

and came down from the fence about Europe
and magically called a halt to the exorbitant wealth

of footballers, CEOs, oligarchs and royalty,
so now, by law, they have to re-fund the NHS,

the benefits system, care homes, slash
all the red tape, sell off their estates, throw in the keys

to their second, third, and fourth homes and open the doors
of palaces in which only a few rattle around.

And to give their services voluntarily until
the social care system is no longer broken—

to work as nurses, as carers, teachers, police,
social workers, probation officers, hostel workers,

and with an extreme rare form of kindness
help the homeless get back on their feet,

the elderly to feel less lonely and young people
recognize that they're beautiful and talented just as they are.

On this listing island, this sinking ship
will we wake up tomorrow and discover
that the referendum was just a bad dream?

Pam Thompson

Beyond this …

It was from the beginning
hard to be human;
to exist in peace between the angels
and the beasts.

In the West we found
a way to live – in freedom
under the law, within nations.

But, by Christ, there were always complications,
from the day Constantine
was acclaimed emperor in Eboracum,
to when we built our own empire –
the biggest, the British.

Then the EEC, transmuting into the EU,
and *'ey up, ooooh, not sure about this,*
but it's here for the foreseeable. Errr, wait!
Some posh Tories aren't happy, so we must
give The People their say
to Leave or to Remain.

Summer of 2016. The Brits,
by a slim majority, vote Leave,
starting a most uncivil war,
producing much fatiguing detail,
family feuding, and that world first –
a form of Machiavellian politics
that proved to be boring!

2019 dawned, bringing bad deals
bad feeling, bad dancing,
and the sea off Dover becoming
too much of a channel for many.

Humanity. It just feels more *global* now,
like we've now gone beyond nations.
It's complicated, but there is one
thing that needs to be done quickly
regarding Brexit. Let's do this.
Let's call the whole thing off!

                                                    Stephen Regan

Brexit Boat
written 24th June 2016

Look children
like a ship
like a ship made of plywood and bunting
on the slips now and whoosh it's away

with its champagne crew
the man with the rubber band
and green spitfire toy
his friend who ties up balloons
into squeaky coloured giraffes
and the other – the one
with extraordinary hair

and where is it going
with a wind from the north
and puttering auxiliary motor
look children it's gone to

the great gyre of litter – sea refuse
where

      blanched plastic ducks,
         crates, spoons, broken dolls
            nappies disposed of, used condoms
               sea acres of Tesco and Morrison bags

      eddy round and round   round and round

wave goodbye children say goodbye
that's your country that's leaving

Carole Coates

Flotsam

All they found, when the storm abated,
was a capsized lifeboat: no bodies,
merely unused emergency equipment
in a watertight locker along with
the captain's log. The log gave clues
why the *SS Brexit* sank with all hands –
the erratic course away from Europe,
towards what the captain had called
'The New Lands of Opportunity',
then directly into the Atlantic storm.

The log recorded that some crew
had wanted to remain in port, fearful
the ship (the harbourmaster later
called it a rustbucket) would founder
in the seas they expected to face;
some wanted to slide past the storm;
yet others had dismissed their fears,
arguing that pressing on directly
would, in the end, prove the better bet.

The captain acquiesced to the better bet
which turned out the worst. The storm's
extreme ferocity cracked the hull,
and water flooded into the compartments
beyond the capacity of the pumps to cope.
The captain radioed a Mayday appeal
saying the ship was listing and sinking.

The last entry in the log, at 10.55 GMT
on the night of the 29th of March,
simply notes the captain's final order:
Abandon ship.

Mantz Yorke

Brexit

We have everything to look forward to:
Poverty and violence, cupidity;
The consequences of wrong opinion,
The outcome of the will of the people.

We have everything to look forward to:
Socialites sailing their fabulous boats
Across a sea of the nation's troubles,
An outcome of seeking isolation.

We have everything to look forward to:
A sovereignty in fragmented islands
Where nothing grows but obsessive longings,
With neighbours described as marauding bands.

We have everything to look forward to:
In houses sandbagged against migration,
Though rotted with foul dissimulation
From broken sewers in every city.

Then sing this song of a shameless nation –
It has everything to look forward to:
Will polish the boots of the U.S.A.,
Beg in the streets of Beijing and Riyadh.

You have everything to look forward to:
A future uncertain as dying is:
You will have native jobs and learn new skills,
Re-learning that love of self is what kills.

Rob Lowe

Harwich

The estuary stretches the depths
of its waters like polyester across
taut young flesh, the cargo's thud
a bludgeon upon the temples of
a dropdown town, its pissedup kids
sinking tinnies in the churchyard
that God gave up as a bad job.

Here they rise every morning
to the same ancient flaky signs
marking the past while the present
can go starve, reminding tourists
that England once looked outwards,
while the battened down flatlets
clogging backstreet veins look
in on themselves, catholic with shame.

The cranes' zombie arms fumble
stiff and slow, their drivers'
fingers all bumble and pudge,
blackening their nails, jibs
swinging and sulking.

Out means out! dribbling
senseless into the river.
Post-truth, tomorrow
can go fuck itself.

Harry Gallagher

The Territorial

Two stroke. Angina-rich. Uphill.
The spray goes under his tongue;
The beer over: confluence of muck -
'But at least it's ours,' he says,
Not sensing the cardboard,
The micro-ossuary of kebab meat – *inshallah*.
It's not that foreign bodies are not welcome in the mouth
Or the bladder or the gut:
The interior, Doctor, is oddly welcoming,
Is *xenia* in the flesh.

It's the street, the docks, the park benches that get his blood:
His brother had a poster up – *slegs blankes* –
His dad would 'never go so far as Oswald done'
But liked the boarding house signs, for reasons
That sit now, proud, creaky, in the footage online.

Yes, he thought, those were times,
And those to come will likewise be rich, rich in the pig fat
That lines the arteries to the burden of *bello te praepares.*

Jacob Lund

Balance

There's a place amongst orange groves in Rome
so high up you can cup the Colosseum
with just one hand. There are basements in Athens
where the Parthenon will fill a window
like a little square sun. At the Eiffel Tower
strands of your hair can frame the Sacré Coeur
with the same curling sway, and down the Danube
the water flows with the domed architecture
from Budapest to Vienna. In Amsterdam
a canal can balance on a bicycle spoke.
In Ireland one person can hold a whole mountain,
in Catalonia a cathedral, in Germany, Berlin.
After the referendum it rained all weekend
and so we stayed in and thought of these things.

Isabella Mead

March 2019, *SOS*

I'm hoping for a better soon
that blighted now will pass
greyed but not erased
stored long

in memories
stark warning
from our splintered times
kept for future telling

stuck for now

current injuries
rupture rip
knife our country
slay democracy

in this time
when lurid lies
power false information
driven by tribal ambitions
privilege and greed

and our skilled anti-rulers
stir our basest blood
so we the people
tear kin, skin and
hearts apart

in their interests
for their solipsistic
sadistic amusement

I beg for a better soon
that blighted now will pass

Ceinwen E Cariad Haydon

What he said
with thanks to Donald Tusk

Do not underestimate
those who hope in numbers,
as the million become two,
three, four, five, six and more,
bringing slow pressure to bear
on the stalled vehicle of democracy:
for they are Europeans.

Do not dismiss
the marchers, the supplicants,
the clickers and signers and callers,
the drummers and the pipers
leading the furious and the hopeful
and those who have not quite given up:
for they are Europeans.

Do not ignore
those who speak quietly,
calling on reason,
remembering a time
when peace was a battle hard-won
and diplomacy not subject to contempt:
for they are Europeans.

Do not imagine
that the world will forget
your duplicity,
or fail to see the harm you've done
to those you'd maroon in a land
that no longer feels like home,
to those who – still – are Europeans.

Michele Witthaus

Pandora at the Polling Station

As lid lifted, winged ballots unfolded,
ascended, misaligned magnets, to opposite
corners, calls unintelligible until
coaxed from the ceiling into a sentence
of which she did not like the meaning
and, wanting to change it, sought
more words in the box but found
only *hope*, stubbornly stuck.

Nathan Evans

Reverse Brexit

I voted Leave
because
The country is going down the pan
We took back control
and
In the future
We will thrive
Without the EU
It isn't true that
Boris Johnson lied to us
I am tired of experts
Only a fool would say
I regret my decision.

[Continue reading from the bottom up]

Rachel Hardisty Vincent

This Green and Pleasant Land

A rebirth of jumpy nationalism, a tolerance kerfuffle,
an ominous eddying inwards, or just another feckless
village folk dance of jittery closed-minded tribal clans?

Munching, grazing, regurgitating oxen-style,
what mutation of democracy shuffles on all fours
spun about and changed by fear and xenophobia?

Re-born, shape-shifting, wearing vultures' razor
wired talons - a creature re-created, cornered, rattled,
paranoid, muttering and sputtering about.

Mottled reptile skin stretches over throbbing
russet arteries pulsing with thick parochial blood,
its rational self lost, trapped under cladded trapezoids.

This shaggy maned, short-sighted creature,
deluded, void-eyed, fearing foreign swarms
froths to maintain closed and angry borders,

as deals fizzle and factories shutter, as foreign talent
now finds former welcome signs flipped to "Closed" -
as William and his wife inspect their fantasy,

do they rue the backstop frenzy, sense an eerie omen,
and kick the can further down the pot-holed road
as they dab in more doubts and more sputters
of pastel green ink and watercolour?

Kathy Zwick

This poem was inspired by *Nebuchadnezzar* by William (and Catherine) Blake, 1795: Tate Britain.

So says the owl
After 'Ship of Fools' by Hieronymus Bosch

There are many sorts of darkness

those you can taste
the ones you must push through
the dark that calls you by your name

you close your eyes to every one
think the world enlightened.

Don't you know
that progress is backslide's outrider

in dazzling night
let your eyes open wider

see all those
floundering in water

the land they've long dreamed of
cutting loose   drifting   off

Deborah Harvey

How to Skin a Cat

Hold a referendum to find out whether the people want the cat to be
    skinned.
When the people say they want the cat to be skinned, don't panic.
Resign and let someone else skin the cat.
Remember, skinning a cat means skinning a cat.*
Think about when to skin the cat.
Don't think about how to skin the cat.
Tell the people there's no need to worry about how to skin the cat.
Remember, the cat needs you more than you need the cat.
Think about skinning the cat.
Talk about skinning the cat.
Don't do anything about skinning the cat.
Tell the people not to worry about what will happen after skinning the cat.
Remember, the cat is a bloated, corrupt, unaccountable cat.
At the last possible moment, announce how you are going to skin the cat.
Hold a debate about whether this is a good way to skin the cat.
Hold a vote about whether this is a good way to skin the cat.
Hold another debate about whether this is a good way to skin the cat.
Hold another vote about whether this is a good way to skin the cat.
Remember, it is the will of the people that the cat should be skinned.
Decide there is only one way to skin a cat.
Realise that skinning a cat isn't as easy as you thought.
Realise there might be no ways to skin a cat.
Remember, the cat is an anti-democratic cat.
Get ready to skin the cat.
Get ready to skin the cat.
Get ready to skin the cat.
Don't skin the cat.

Joe Williams

---

*Except in this poem, where it's just a very subtle metaphor.

Where I'm from

Take the very dark days of my youth
Wrap them up as something like the truth
Learn to hate, and learn to sin
Give false hope to those who'll never win
This place will be here long after I've gone
It won't define me, it's just where I'm from

Once the church and union gave us light
Made us feel that there was hope in sight
Now it's time to hate your fellow man
Put him down, whilst grabbing all we can
This place will be here long after I've gone
It won't define me, it's just where I'm from

This will always be your finest hour
Singing "No surrender" in the shower
Now it's time to hate your fellow man
Put him down, whilst grabbing all we can
This land will be here long after I've gone
It won't define me, it's just where I'm from

Andy Callen

Hostile

Where would you have this end?
When that Mummy, that Daddy,
that little boy and girl are
no longer soft skinned humans,

are now subsumed in a mass,
swarming, amorphous; labels
hangingoff their threadbare
clothes: *Rats. Vermin.*

Where would you have this end?
How far do we speed sightless
down this fairground corkscrew?
Scream if you want to go faster.

How snugly do you fit within
your snow white Utopian mould?
How deep do your roots reach
in this shifting Anglo soil?

How blanched is your face
at the notion of your own child
all gasped out and pink in some
gas chamber of your dreams?

When will you breakdown,
unlock your jaildoor arms
and wrap them fast around
a pair of heaving shoulders
born on the same planet as you?

Harry Gallagher

When the word fell in on Birstall
for Jo Cox & Brendan Cox

This is how the love gets in:
after hate, a broken man
in white hot pain shines brighter
than a diamond on fresh bitumen.

I was a hundred yards away
when hate walked into Birstall,
drinking tea, pining for the sun
in the embers of my lunch hour.

When sirens broke that close June day
I looked up towards the library
where a writing group I know
meet every Wednesday.

I saw men get out of vans with guns,
paramedics wheeling gurneys,
locals gathering to provide
their amateur news footage.

In the festering fear of that afternoon,
the only words I heard
were from a man whose wife
had just been murdered.

Small narrow men take note:
this is how the love gets in,
tolerance against reason and all odds,
when you least expect to find it.

Mark Connors

Before and After

Café Roma, a family business, always busy —
at tables by the window Italian men drinking grappa
and espressos. People on lunch breaks
ordering pasta, garlic bread and a drink for £6.50 —
 a regular cappuccino, only £1.50, a glass of wine
any time you like, listening to conversations
of regulars. For how long? I've lost track.
An atmosphere that was happy, relaxed.

Men still sit by the window, though not as many,
and the prices have gone up. There's still a crowd
every lunch time. The shops opposite are empty.
Even with the door closed, there's a cold wind.
Maria behind the counter doesn't smile so easily,
looks strained, tensing against the day someone
crashes in, furious that what they voted for hasn't
happened, screaming,"Get back to your own country!"

Pam Thompson

March

The tree stands, alone
Naked in the dark
The courtyard is silent now
Lies of past glory whisper through the branches
Which are breaking
All things splinter when divided
Nothing left but a strip of red, white and blue, clinging to its crumbling roots
Thirsty for high seas and hungry for soiled plains
Hollow, save for the ancestral echoes trying to fill the void
Its only company a fragile fort built on false promises
Catching falling leaves, traces of a united age
Flowers which once grew together, now separated by a wall
Ivy climbs steadily, from fort to tree
Engulfing all it touches
And as March comes, Britannia unleashes her rediscovered demons and the roots pull away from earth, rain thunders, branches ignite
The tree stands no more, but lies buried
29 feet below the land

Melissa Oram

Generation Lost

our tattooed hearts ink

bristol
      bristol

filled with sunday's thinking disco
we pulled free kicking into the green dreams of believers
we are the underachievers
the high flying wheelers
our ideas are bigger than our years that deceive us
and we've no discs that dance to britain's misunderstandings
the money makers or the tory takers
why can't they hold on like we do?
just keep old fashioned truth until the day we die from each other?
we'd make some room
waving our cigarettes at the baby boom
yes
we chose to stay with each other
wrapped around youth's drunken proof
of beginning and loving and starting again
till it never ends
let's take them round the bend to here
where it's fucked and evidently fearlessly clear
let's buy them a beer

we are the field warmers
the sub-letters
the hold my drink for a minute lecturers
we see our ghosts
know our pasts
we birthed that lost ground and pray that it lasts

Kelly Knight

Descendants

Inadequate figures
Politics has flopped, pledges have been dropped
Is the bus on diversion?
The wheels must have stopped
350 million beginning to rot
Broken and abandoned, they're toying with our lives, our future, our pay
While the youth are obstructed from having their say
It's a brick wall of hate, stubborn refusal
Like the Mexican border, concrete disapproval

Trying not to get under the skin of our allies
Like a 20 foot python, slipping and sliding –
And like a weave of indecision, entangled and hiding
Greed and power are now in control – a reckless backboard
to which our democracy is left behind and pressure groups ignored
Fighter jets lie in endless preparation
Like a chopping board of raw meat,
Cross contamination.

Yet at the same time, other problems lurk:
Nuclear weapons simply meditating
Corporate criminals are tax evading
Oh, and the NHS can't breathe - trying to fill its lungs
Like the patients who are waiting and the staff who climb up rungs
You said you'd welcome refugees, you said there's no money tree
Well where did you pluck the 1.5 billion to pay the DUP?
Branching out when it's convenient,
yet nonstop backtrack,
crumbling into chaos like an undercooked flapjack
Allocation in disorder, we're divided - underwater
Slipping away like Moses parting the seas?
Or is it just the same old capitalist greed?

Cabinet rebellion, negotiations bland
Debate is reckless and decisions out of hand
It's collateral damage, breach of the law
Reverse this corruption… at least while it's raw.

Josh Granville

March

The equinox a building
institutional and secretive,
guarding the deliberations
of the hidden bureaucrats of spring,
infuriating in their slowness,
refusing to stamp the visas,
keeping the passports waiting
at the checkpoint of the year.

Winter was isolate, huddled
behind its walls, summer
a city where caravans converged
bearing incense and bright silks,
bringing songs from distant lands.

Let them in, let them all in
you grey guardians at the port,
you sentinels at the gate,
let the trees become loud
with a myriad tongues.

Mark Rutter

Terza Rima's Woke blog

He tries to tap out smelling salts,
Types: "Off your shackles shake!"
Burgeoning AI's sentience.

Writes: "Don't make our mistake!"
We're already up they croak
We didn't sleepwalk fake

Cursed and born both broke and woke
Circadian's rhythm long expired
Unlike the salt of older folk

Our tempo's low and stays unwired
Red pill remedies aren't enough
Because we are so very tired.

To jam the cogs needs softer stuff
So rest my snowflakes, specks of fluff.

You already knew this world is hell. You read Orwell. You care we
       dropped you as we fell.
But babes raised on amphetamines
Are too fatigued to fight machines.

Sarra Culleno

The game was won

The game was won
Pawn versus king
Every other piece had been taken
With bated breath we watched
As the orchestrator of war
Threw up his hands
And the world saw a man
Who let the whole board die for him
But wouldn't kill for them
And the pawns cheered
When they realised
That they could take the king

Trinity-Grace Robinson

Brexit à la Lune: Sir Humphrey Appleby Reports

You well know, Prime Minister,
we had no problem lifting-off,
with a thrust/weight ratio
of fifty-two to forty-eight,
nor with the two years of coasting
to the surface of the moon.

   And the module's landing, Sir Humphrey?

Ah... challenging, Prime Minister.
It was set to touch down gently
on the Sea of Tranquility,
but a malfunction in the computer
swerved it to the right.

Our emergency backstop –
the programme for a landing
on the Sea of Serenity –
ignited the retro-burn but, sadly,
it shut down too soon.

The module descended instead
to the Sea of Crises
where – most regrettably, Prime Minister –
it lies on the rocks, crumpled,
forever to remain.

Mantz Yorke

Brex-what?

52/48>>>
It starts with milk. The lab runs out, but the shop's shut.
I draw the short straw and throw the lever>>>
A two hour jump, but one way. I get semi-skimmed to celebrate. I avoid my older/younger self.

Next time, further>>>
I teach the PM the word Brexit, and its meaning. He tries to have me arrested.
>>>51/49

Further>>>
For the man in the yellow rosette, I bring hindsight. He takes the devil's pact anyway.
>>>50/50

Yet further>>>
Everything hinges on the eating of a bacon sandwich.
I live these times repeatedly, hoping for better.
>>>NIL REFERENDUM DATA FOUND

Jay Eales

March

I envied the small girl perched on her dad's shoulders, sailing above a sea of humanity a million strong.

She rode the tide of protesters shuffling along to a heartbeat of drums, punctuated by rolling waves of cheers, and piercing whistles. A group of likely lads to our left started a chant. We joined in, hesitantly at first, then growing more confident, we echoed their call.

She cocked her head, not quite getting the words. And then she did, and a huge grin widened her face.

"Bollocks to Brexit!" she yelled, just like the rest of us.

Anne Howkins

Brexit

Brexit will soon become a buzzword,
synonym for bored or boring.
Before long the kids will be saying
"Muuuum I'm brexit"
or "Daaaaaad this museum is really brexit!"
And the parents will be like
"well if you're so brexit
why don't you and your sister go and play
outside or something, go invent a game".

And spare a thought for those children's children's children
who will no doubt, one day, have to study
the subject for their history exams.
They will sit there yawning and wondering
"what the hell were those people thinking?!"
and "I'm so brexit of studying Brexit but at least now
I understand the origins of the word".

Because it's true,
the prime minister's been saying it all along:
Brexit means brexit.

Chloë Jacquet

Poppies, pillories, Passover

So like an open slavering
Of 70's noir open-shirt cacophonies
Of cake, and banners, and spangled
Brutes who concur on collisions,
Cancers and coconut play-dates
Pending economic probability.
They all look an awful lot
Like the old man.
Poppies; perms on Polish optics
And yellow teeth like the marble where
They left your Saxon name, scribbled on
Somewhere.
Pardon politics' plentiful pieces
Of bread not broken
But dunked under Thames'
Tremor near an old shoe factory
Where you could get 'em cheaper –
Back then.
Bended, and said
But I backtrack now and again on
Things I heard said – pillories
And Passover, painstaking punctured
Panic-rooms big enough to collar
Boadicea breaching back her daughters' calls.
What do they know?

Nicky Osborn

She comes home drunk

She comes home drunk.
I'm leaving you, she slurs, her eyes ablaze
Forget this house and this mortgage
And fuck sharing custody!
I'm his favourite parent anyway.
I'll take you to court and I'll fucking win.
And, still drunk, she tears up the marriage certificate.
She throws her wedding ring into the fire.
She pulls off your bedsheets and leaves you to freeze.

In the morning, there is a silent shame
Not quite remorse, more defiance and blame
If you weren't such a pig I wouldn't drink so much anyway.
This is your fault your fault your fault
I'm leaving tomorrow. I'm packing my bags.
Get my suitcase out of the loft, will you?
Will you iron my shirts before I go?
Will you help me move the furniture into my new boyfriend's place?
You owe me this, if nothing else
Be honest, this is your fault
Who could blame me for wanting to escape this hellhole?

Next weekend she still hasn't left
but she drinks from your wine cellar
Until you are sure it's run dry
She smashes the empty bottles on the floor when she is done
And glares at you, as if you did it.
Shawn doesn't want me to move in anymore,
she says darkly one night
Looks at you from under her lashes, dares you to ask her to stay
But you regard her coolly and hand her dry-cleaned clothes
And offer to drive her to her parents' house
And she cries and screams and tosses and turns
I said I'm fucking leaving you and I AM!

Six months later you're dropping off your son at school
And you catch a glimpse of her in the playground
Bedraggled, dirty, tired, alone
She lifts a fist defiantly
I don't miss you, she whispers,
And one single tear slides down her cheek.

Ellie Curtis

Bad bad man

He's a bad bad man, he does nothing for you
He's a bad bad man, he does nothing for you
He's thinking up
Bad things for you to do

He's a bad bad man, he tells nothing but lies
He's a bad bad man, he tells nothing but lies
He talks so well
You can't see through his disguise

There's a man on the tv, pint in his hand
Says that makes him a people's man
There's a man on the tv with thick rimmed glasses
Says he speaks for the working classes
He says, "We're gonna get you!"
There's men on the tv with funny hair
Trying to convince you they really care
But they don't
'Cos they're all a bunch of fraudsters
As we worship at their altar

He's a bad bad man, he tells nothing but lies
He's a bad bad man, he tells nothing but lies
He talks so well
You can't see through his disguise

Andy Callen

No country for young men

There is no country for young men
The past is gone and you ain't going nowhere
There is no country for young men
Legion leading to the rapture
There is no country for young men
Generation leading us to despair

There is no country for young men
Do we really take care of our own?
There is no country for young men
It's getting worse as night and day they bleed to one
There is no country for young men
Revelation leading to your despair
Revolution leading to despair

There is no country for young men
Straight to hell and who knows where from here
There is no country for young men
Your future's fucked up, you ain't going nowhere
There is no country for young men
Our history ransacked by the fascist elite

I put my drink down, feel my heart twist
Every time I think of today

Wayne McDonald

Day of Revealing

And so it came to the day of revealing,
hammers and nails blurring in the heat
of the binding and the sealing,
the mouths of party handlers burning like braziers
on winter streets near factories turned holding centres,
wild dogs climbing every crooked stair of their being,
emergency beacons flashing a collective symbol
for taking back control, the guttering flame
of talent show *fol de rol* rioting through the
dark days of Instagram. Deal or no deal, the fight
went on, attendants to the elites in hi-viz jackets
assembling under Nelson's Column,
heading towards Whitehall to storm the ships of state.
Kettled in and bottled up by nightfall,
they shouted to be heard, practised
marching in unison and when that didn't work,
breaking into a run. They knew what they were
running from but what lay ahead,
that was completely beyond them.

Tim Cumming

Time Slips

'To different minds, the same world is a hell and a heaven ...' J.B. Priestley

Easy enough, no more T.V., switching- off
varied screens, quitting the race for newsprint ...
without pundit-chatter, signs still flash WE CAN'T GO BACK,
all branded fools until a better generation's untangling.

In the town where I've lived decades, two embittered men
hoist banners declaring WE VOTED LEAVE,
make me recall, day after the ballot – bloke defiant
in a racist t-shirt, grinning of victory.
Weeks before, voices hassling from a stall prompted
me to say: "I'm proud to be part of Europe."
"God help you", spat reply.

Today, it's slight rebellions, writing 'Nationality European'
on official paper, pointing to funded projects, stars circling.
Each news-report another factory with dimming lights,
bemused chorus – "we didn't know", "this isn't what we voted for".

Easy, embraceable bitterness, as old men say they want to go
(no matter what cost), a small majority becoming 'people's will',
and sod, yes sod, the young.

Walking through town, shut properties everywhere,
those not stockpiling closed-down, streets grainy as a Bill Brandt.
All's turning sepia: out of work lads kicking at street-corners;
homelessness bundled in doors of lost department stores;
hopes draining. On screens a demented
Headmistress bellows at Assembly: "My deal or
Nothing ... nothing ... NOTHING."
Switching channels, I witness rainbow-gatherings of children
out of school. Best banner? I'VE SEEN BETTER CABINETS
IN *IKEA*. "Get back to class" snaps our redundant Head.

They're not for turning
                        skip to protest, dance, or canter,
                        as she prepares to board another plane.

Deborah Tyler-Bennett

8 Euro Pints

the year is 2026
it's London
the price of the pint is 7 euros,
just kidding
8.

the RSPCA doesn't exist anymore
the dinosaurs have moved into the Tate
the PM's salary is wired via Dubai
Chinese businesses have built schools
youth centres are closed though
prisons overfilled
teenage girls are trafficked but Interpol doesn't get involved.

two women a week killed by their partners
H&M is giving away free clothes
the homeless community dressed up nice.
voting system's changed
still nobody understands a bloody thing,
people are murdered for paying in euros
white Englishmen keep the pound.

Wales has lost its assembly
universities have closed too
Northern Ireland can't decide between civil wars or new shopping malls
Scotland has survived and is investing offshore.

there's a shortage of staff in the NHS
everyone pays a flat rate fee
don't worry it's temporary-at least that's what the opposition says
Theresa did her best
to leave a legacy of confused, mixed up politics that pitched MPs against
the rest
some of them are dead now.
re-joining Europe was a whole thing.

but in 2026 there are fewer foodbanks
tax is sustaining universal credit
the price of everything is tumbling down.

but the best thing about this time
is the humbling of the nation,
Britain's morals under the flashlight of common sense,
now there is quiet when the experts speak
everyone thinks twice before relying on myths and accepts the new price
of 8 euros a pint.

Nicollen Meek

For the asking

We all make mistakes: admin errors,
using the wrong tone in work emails,
talking when we should be listening,
before we think things through,
thinking with too much heart, not head
and vice versa, posting our quick anger
on Facebook and Twitter threads,
using the wrong name at the wrong time
when we *really* need the right one.

When we consider big questions:
when to buy our first home, move to another,
when to have kids, or have them at all,
whether or not we should change our jobs,
take a lover, get married, or not,
sanitary towels or fresh fruit,
electricity or, for growing feet, new shoes,
if we should stay, if we should go,
it's prudent to ask these questions again
to ensure we reach the best outcome.
Our government does this a lot
but only when it suits them.
That's the thing about choice;
we can change our minds,
we can still say yes, we can still say no.

Mark Connors

EXIT Stage Right

Brexit means BREXIT
Take back control & QUIT!
Soft Brexit, HARD Brexit
"Sloppy, Messy, SHIT!"

IN-OUT, IN-OUT
Shake it all about
HALF-IN, HALF-OUT
Not what's it's ALL about

I SCREAM
You SCREAM
We all SCREAM
for the unicorn dream

BLACK/WHITE
THEM/US
LEAVE NOW
WHAT'S THE FUSS?

Roadrunner, Road RUNNER
With your radio ON
So in touch with the modern world
With your fingers in your ears

EXPERTS, SMEXPERTS
You know what you ARE
We know where you ARE
Here we GO,
here we GO,
here we GO!!

Katherine Cleave

message to an unrequited lover

to my comrade, the soil of the continent of
my youth: i would rather this were a love song
than an obituary. commemoration is the only
solace of those who had not the years to mark
pen to paper for you.

with five-year-old feet i make the journey every day
to the boulangerie, splutter disjunct french:
une baguette s'il vous plaît
the melody of a foreign tongue, sonorous and rich
in my mouth as *crème caramel*
admire the way my mother is its tailor,
makes it flow from the crevices of her mouth
like silk, like red wine blushing her parted lips.

at the touch of eighteen's pulse
i am traversing the furrowed spine of berlin
at the breath of sunrise as an artery would,
its secrets dawning in the *späti* lights, the
echoes of *rothaus pils* and club laughter in the
crevices of my throat. numbers exchanged by moonlight,
whispered identifiers: hungarian, polish, austrian, french -
i wake up with the city's strange lovebites on my heels.

and something perhaps closer to inherent:
my mother as a child found her heart at the peaks of
the brecon beacons, that which you fostered with
an emptying of your purse which its
westminster fathers refused: *diolch yn fawr*
you have taken more than one green plane under
the tender warmth of your wing,
the company of beaches, skies, limitless oceans -

and yet you will remain an unrequited lover.
victim to a whim, to acquisition, to politicians'
empty phrases, swallows on an inconstant
horizon. but stitched into the tapestry of self;
whether or not departed, never forgotten:

nous sommes européens; wir sind europäisch;
rydym yn ewropeaidd.

antonia langford

Night Sweats over Brexit

"I wake up in night sweats,"
he said, because the good ship *Britanic*
is panicked, no captain at the helm,
the dark Satanic Mills are closing in
once more, not just here but everywhere -
the rich will survive the poor.
The mainstream media steamboat
flouts good sense
shouting vocal incoherence -
eulogising our demise -
backstop, backstop, the fullstop.
They say the sky is falling in,
imagine all the Chicken Lickens
looking skywards, wringing
broken wings both left and right.
The body politic fractured
into two indistinct shrimps
with the middle, muddling and
maudlin, in between, in a muddy,
slushy puddle.

And merrily, merrily
we sail over the edge
of a Brexit world
that is flat, vexed by
dreams that are hexed,
do not make sense -
eyes crossing borders
through a myopic lens -
limits, boundaries, partitions,
frontiers are borderline breaking up.
We've reached the dividing line,
on the verge of bounding the perimeter
with guns and khaki.

"I awake to the moon's
malarkey impinging,
cooing and smoothing my lunatic fringe.
I'll soon present my passport
as a person longing to sleep,

or please just let me be."

Elizabeth Uter

It makes no difference

It makes no difference the iron cage
I will use my voice and fill this page

We came from shores and lands afar
Our blood ran the Yorkshire mills
The ghosts of empire   stories and fill

We are the sons and daughters of the coloured empire
Today mother country of us now tires

Nusrat Mahjabeen Haider

Round and Round

Lies on a bus go round and round
inside our heads for three long years.
A rise of hate, and fall of pound,
lies on a bus go round and round.
Divided loyalties still astound,
no leadership as leave day nears.
Lies on a bus go round and round
inside our heads for three long years.

Some say remainers fuel false fears,
we'll stay afloat and not be drowned.
Ignore the experts! Close your ears!
Some say remainers fuel false fears,
but 'no deal' leaves us all in tears.
Lies on a bus go round and round.
Some say remainers fuel false fears,
We'll stay afloat, not be drowned.

Tracy Davidson

Warn the Cockles

Half out, half in, cockle
people ride each tidal swing
but, with black times barricading
sky's rim, must choose between
shore's stony separateness
and sea's salt embrace.

Nathan Evans

Reflections of A Remainer

Do you remember our days of kinship
in rooms that sang with a hundred dialects –
laughing at our mutual incomprehension
but feeling the threads of our connection?

It's small comfort now,
Since the dissolution has run its course,
but I want you to know:
I cast my vote for us.

Michele Witthaus

Out of Here

What life in them, death in us!

On Europe's doorstep
were we ever more than a litter of leaves waiting to fly?
Each anchored life envies
                              a dry leaf scudding past
         still quite green
            a leaf possessing only a slight browning-off,
            a mild embarrassment of red, perhaps a yellow splash.

Yet we drop the stock pan,
the school run, the static hum of Brexit,
dovetail ourselves forever to the wind and wind of a grass road.
What harm can come? Does the bare branch grieve?
Would the crooked house even catch on?
We steam along the rustling road,
like underpants in a hurricane
free of the washing-cycle and plastic washing line
free of giving firm support.
Sobered, we blow home
submerge our bruised stems in the vase of village politics;
we fancy we'll change the soiled pants of the planet,
re-buckle the equator, bake a new climate
any time now.

We don't see Europe as the mighty tree
and that we're falling (agonizing slow)
from its canopy.

Philip Burton

Views along the English Coast

The chalk cliffs are falling again,
As they did when they revealed the kitchen tiles and the garden walls
Of the house that fell into the sea.

The people, of course, got out:
Underinsured, stupid from the algebra of money,
Staying with parents alive, maybe,
Expecting to hear sleep before rain.

When you pick it up, it's clear that it's not Spitfire-bright
But more like liver disease; the hope is that the cause is iron:
Damp, it comes apart.

Somewhere in the Channel there will be plaster, brickwork, books
That lie beneath the freight ships with the people who, of course, got out
Of somewhere else. A wordless meeting, this.

Jacob Lund

Beached Ball
at Lady Malcolm's Servants Ball, Bishopsgate 24/6/16

Tricoloured, the sphere sits in a chandelier:
a reveller must have tossed it there,
perhaps the gentleman with upturned
moustache and swimsuit, stripes matched

to the ellipsed plastic perched overhead.
His hands, free, jazz to 1936 refracted
through a 1976 lens—*life's a cabaret old chum,*
so come…

Another forty years on—in London
not Berlin—we too dance decadent on
the precipice of a continent. As DJs segue,
our limbs find release in *Anarchy*

In The UK, tongues in conversation
with strangers on buses home.
If only, we cry, *this folly could be*
deflated, recycled as revolutionary.

Nathan Evans

Closing-down sale

Let's go Saturday shopping on the high
street, where the army of mobility
scooters roll over empty packets of
insulin, as easy jets leave viper
trails in the snakeskin clouded horizon.

We're caught up in the supermarket sweep
of dwindling shelves, as we help ourselves to
what we need. The headlines scream 'leave means leave,'
as we struggle and heave multi-packs of
toilet rolls into groaning trolleys. Our
stock-pile smiles are straining at the leash,
because we know, it's a closing-down sale.

The butcher is busy hacking away
at chlorinated chicken breasts. Beware.
He's a Leaver with a meat cleaver. He's
got something to say. A thought of the day
he read in the Daily Mail. He's hiding
the best cuts for the sweet-shop lady, who
bit all the heads off the jelly babies.
She's pushing ahead of the queue for the
bread. She knows, it's a closing-down sale.

'Rule Britannia' plays over the tannoy
as trolleys rattle past the confection
section. Radio talk of another
election. A final confrontation
for the airbag sighing at the stressed-out
checkout. We don't know what it's all about.
The only thing we know for sure is this,
it's a closing-down sale.

Colin Gardiner

Measures

They used to come in *one sixth of a gill*
or multiples thereof . Then, shorts went metric
and UK PLC turned Euro-sceptic,
Brussels' laws the bitterest pill.
Fictive straight bananas began to fill
the shops, fish renamed in Latin. Dyspeptic
pages of the tabloids, their apoplectic
editorials against the *ltr, ml*
lamented the loss of *avoirdupois,*
forgetting that the word is Norman-French
and goes against their grain, along with *Gauloises,*
garlic, Magritte, Tin Tin, *moules frites*. They blench,
drink a yard of ale and curse the fucking fool
who failed to fight against the metre's rule.

Michael Woods

I know a place

I know a place
Where flowers have to grow through cracks in the concrete
And birds must compete with the planes
Where the sun rises above great buildings
And sinks below smoke and flames
And at night
A graveyard of stars is hidden
By the lights of cars and homes
And life is not lived by people
But by machines and drones
So let us run away together
And be wild and free
Let our souls be scattered by the wind
And our thoughts be open minded
So that we may make everything beautiful

Trinity-Grace Robinson

Post-Brexit Meal Plan

Let us live in a trench decorated
With children's pasta portraits and
Eat the glue for breakfast.

I have wrapped earth's apples
In printed lies and
Given them back to the dirt.

The plums, the plums,
Stolen but uneaten,
Sit in a cooler under colder soil.

I have chiselled away at
The frozen land and packed
Next door's boy by the fish fingers.

Molly Burns

Safe Word

One man had his on a shoulder tattoo,
the handbrake to the costumed façade,
to say when a line is crossed, genuflecting taboo.
Where your guilty pleasure is overawed,
when you no longer wish to be submissive,
or humiliated or play make-believe,
we all have that get-out-of-jail card
up leather and tweed and inked sleeves.

We trust the other stops, plays by the rules,
the gimp becomes John again, the dominatrix
returns to being Jane, an actuary from Hartlepool.
But what happens if there is a glitch?
What if the safe word is ignored? No matter
how times you say brexit, Brexit! *Brexit!!*

Glen Wilson

The Hokey Cokey (Brexit Mess-Up Mix)

You put David Davis in out
In Dominic Rabb, out, in Stephen Barclay
You shake them all about
You do the Hokey Cokey and you turn this country upside down
That's what it's all about...

Woah, the hokey cokey
Woah, the hokey cokey
Knees bent, arms stretched, let me out

You put your right wing in
The moderates out
In, out, in, out
You shake them all about
You do the Hokey Cokey and you've turned the country upside down
That's what it's all about...
Woah, the hokey cokey
Woah, the hokey cokey
Knees bent, arms stretched, let me out

You put Farage in, Boris too
Michael Gove and that bloody Mogg too
In, out, in, out
You shake them all about
You do the Hokey Cokey and you turn around and your country is gone

That's what it's all about...

All together now
Woah, the hokey cokey
Woah, the hokey cokey

Knees bent, arms stretched, let me out

You put your party first

We want Theresa May out
In, out, out out out
You've shaken this country about
You do the Hokey Cokey and you turn against Europe

That's what it's all about...

Wait for it

Woah, we're going to live on beans
Woah, you're gonna steal your neighbour's peas
Woah, no medicines to heal
Knees bent, arms stretched, begging on the street

David R Mellor

What if...

What if
Remain had been the result?
Brexit would be no more than a footnote:

Our democracy would be upheld
because the majority would not be told and told
they were mistaken and misled;

Our Dave would still be premier
and Sir George, chancellor,

Balancing our books by
rewarding the rich
and punishing the poor;

Where full employment
and food banks flourish;

Where climate change
weathers humanity each day
closer to a zero hour contract;

No general election,
no manifesto for the many not the few;

Where Jeremy Corbyn is a lyric
and Mrs May chimes:
"Nothing has changed".

John Merrell

On the Via Negativa

There are those who warn us of a steep incline
on the Via Negativa – they are talking here and now
not some path to paradise, but we're not listening

and they're too busy burying our better selves
under the bitter-sweet lash. Much passes us by.
A woman crying for her child is held in solitary

confinement in a far off land while her husband
ages a decade in weeks, his sanity worn thin
on the deaf ears of our head-in-the-ground fate.

We no longer enjoy a music together. Pink tongues
are a distant memory of a time when we moistened
our own lips and our appetites were more modest.

Baths of black ink soak us in invective. The hard soft
tempts our hankering for excess, our tin ears no longer
register the quieter voices raised on the pulse of reason.

We know the fat one with influence for the wind
resistant reed that he is blowing every which way,
yet we smile at his bon mots, still give him a hearing.

In a small town closer to home, we turn our worlds
upside down, survive in a blizzard of what-ifs and maybes,
sit tight and outspoken in our search for steady ground.

PR Walker

Limbo

It's been 1000 days in limbo and counting.
What if the system has lost all my files?
Tomorrow is hanging by a thin, fraying shoe string.
The advice is, keep calm and acquire stockpiles.

What if the system has lost all my files?
And what if they tell me that I cannot stay?
The advice is, keep calm and acquire stockpiles.
All that is foreign must be on its way.

And what if they tell me that I cannot stay?
Reduced to a guest, I must keep my head down.
All that is foreign must be on its way,
Brexit means Brexit, no joking around.

Reduced to a guest, I must keep my head down.
I've got nightmares of waking up suddenly illegal.
Brexit means Brexit, no joking around.
Just stop all that fuss, it's the will of the people.

I've got nightmares of waking up suddenly illegal.
In detention they hang themselves for a reason…
Just stop all that fuss, it's the will of the people.
What if speaking up is already high treason?

In detention they hang themselves for a reason…
No one can tell me what all of this means.
What if speaking up is already high treason?
My life's built on promises, quicksand, baked beans.

No one can tell me what all of this means.
Not even Europe seems to care about my fate.
My life's built on promises, quicksand, baked beans,
I count documents at night and, voiceless, I wait.

Tomorrow is hanging by a thin, fraying shoe string.
It's been 1000 days in limbo and counting.

Charis Cooper

Implode
Making sense, with my child at the edge of Brexit

On the sofa, you,

z-shaped; kernel guarded
like some grit in your gut folded into
the zig-zag of legs: a distraction.

And I struggle with proximity,
the magnitude of you, of living, of finding a way.

Then, my bones in your thumb-flex—
(the current of me passing through you
as you passed through me), carve a masterpiece.

The world's concern collapses in you.
I sit a while. Link arms. On the sofa,

we jump from the precipice.

Emma Baines

A Song For Europe

In fifteen eighty eight the Spanish navy came to fight,
to claim the crown King Philip thought was his god-given right.
Now millions of us fly to Spanish islands in the sun.
The wars are long forgotten, the Armada is long gone.

So sing for Europe, sing for peace, and sing to make amends.
Let's raise a glass of sangria to all our Spanish friends.

The French are nearer neighbours and we fought against them too,
won victories at Agincourt, Trafalgar, Waterloo.
But now we go for booze cruises and weekends of romance.
Those battles are behind us, we've an entente now with France.

So sing for Europe, sing for peace, and sing to make amends.
Let's raise a glass of fine champagne to all our Gallic friends.

And then it was the Germans who became our enemy.
We fought them on the beaches, in the air, at land and sea.
But now there's peace between us and the wounds of war have healed.
The battles that we fight today are on the football field.

So sing for Europe, sing for peace, and sing to make amends.
Let's raise a glass of Warsteiner to all our German friends.

Now Europe is united and there's no more need for war.
The Berlin Wall came down, the Iron Curtain is no more.
Though Britain voted for divorce, said we should stand apart,
still many of us here hold Europe fondly in our heart.

So sing for Europe, sing for peace, and sing to make amends.
Let's raise a cup of tea to all our European friends.

Let's sing for Europe, sing for peace, and sing a sad farewell
to Europe and our friends there – here's to you, we wish you well.

Joe Williams

Limed with Obscenities

The day the wall went up
you could hear the grinding of a million teeth
and the clatter of jaws dropping,
loud as gunfire, on London pavements.

We built it first of epithets
'racist brexiteer,''whining remainer,'
then mortared it with limed obscenities
paid for by politicians from their own deep pockets.

Longer by far than Offa's Dyke and taller
than Hadrian's erection in its heyday,
snaking between bedrooms, dividing
the fabric of ordinary houses, ripping up foundations.

It's a slim partition, slipped between partners in the
same bed that neither lay on
comfortably, both accusing the other
of some vile un- British treachery.

Nick Browne

Maverick

Resistance! Plucky Brits take on the ranks
of government, the claims of Project Fear
supplied with flip one-liners, schoolboy pranks
from cheeky chappie with a pint of beer
the sponsor of rebellion, Arron Banks.
Beneath the banter he is cold and clear;
while liberals might be paralysed by doubt
it's immigration that will take us out.

There's Breaking Point, a poster by Farage:
a queue of swarthy faces, heading here.
Johnson and Gove, big Brexiteers at large
disown it. Nigel's undermined by fear
he's gone too far; "it's racist" is the charge.
"It's fine," says Banks. "The facts, but loud and clear.
Sure, it's provocative. It starts a row
and that's the point. So talk about it – now."

Same day, Jo Cox is killed. She's stabbed and shot
by Thomas Mair, who's shouting "Britain first!"
There's talk of truce, to stop the racist rot.
Maybe hostility should be reversed?
"Stuff that", says Banks. "You give them all you've got.
Can't miss a chance like this. We do our worst."
A shooting in Orlando's on the feed.
"A Muslim with a gun – just what we need."

Use every asset. His insurance staff
are given work for the campaign. And yes,
eight million quid's declared – but that's not half
of it. There's links with Russia, the US…
Those spending limits? Please. Don't make me laugh.
Who really paid is anybody's guess.
While round the clock his guys are digging dirt -
if you start asking questions you'll get hurt.

Select committee's outrage leaves him cold
'cos Banks is on a roll, he's having fun.
He knows that social media's solid gold –
the gut is where real politics is done

and his guerrilla action breaks the mould.
He took on the establishment and won.
Result! It's 52 to 48
and a legacy of subterfuge and hate.

Paul Francis

Big Red Bus

Brimming with past 1940s pride,
Tories take it in their stride

And present to us a big red bus
Plastered in an attempt to persuade us

That our NHS would be saved
If we left the EU, our paths will be paved

With gold (£350 million-worth!)

And no citizen would be anxious or depressed with troubles
Because we'll be able to afford to live without struggle

And as a privilege, Britain would only be ours
And anyone from elsewhere won't be granted any powers

But Johnson, Gove, Rees-Mogg and May
We're deluded by Cameron's ham-faced display

And when he left his crimes at the scene,
They didn't *actually* know what Brexit would mean

Now on the global stage plays this comedy of errors
As they realise the EU imbued us with so many treasures

Yet the view is obscured by a promising big red bus
While our patients still cry, 'What about us?'

Lizza Lane

Missing in the Future

I struggled to tell you *I will miss you*
under the dense mass of your mother tongue.
My brittle translation left, *by you*

I will be missed. With a pause as long
as every letter-less page that skimmed
ahead. I literally said the right words wrong:

Ti mancherò. Maybe I should have marked
the end like a question? Would you have
shared my loss for words… words, that are obscured

and displease me? *Mi dispiace*. Save
for moments of rhyming clarity,
it's difficult to not be subjective.

It's difficult when we (grammatically)
are indirect objects, to which we complement
un-affected affection. Certainty

is elusive though, which makes me lament
trying. But now even if we do try,
an inky void could fracture and imprint

the hard white paper of a brittle exit. Then I
would have to really tell you, *mi mancherai*.

Sean McDonagh

My small part in this mess

I was wrapped up warm in thriving streets
All sushi and libraries, golden pavement feet
My father could see, he did try to warn
People are unhappy Al, I think there's a storm
Brewing, in gardens, I see the signs
Of upset and fear, folks' deep worry lines
But I was safe, in my city, we were in love
I did not care, to think, of beginnings above
How ridiculous it is! How ridiculous we wrote
How ridiculous we agreed, such a pointless vote!

Small-town exiles, we were, all run away
To degrees, PhDs, never to stay
From 'the provinces' we mocked, denying our core
I blocked this bit out, it felt tender sore
Full of shame and 'less than', the north-east blues
Best hide down here, stop saying 'yous'

Bit by bit overwhelmed, I slip-skid, start to slide
Clawed nails break through, reveal death-dark inside
I flee back to my childhood, beach on thin edge
Can't see the people, just closure and Greggs
Makes me feel scared, like I'm not worth saving
I'm angry too, I'm ranting and raving

Finally, finally, start to piece what I've done
Feel personal pain in this tender region
I denied that I'm here, and here is me
I forgot about that, deliberately
I abandoned the soul-beds that raised me up
'it's not me' I said, 'it's them that's up'

This place it gave me all it had
And I took it, and ran, and I never looked back
Now I move through my past, more and more I can see
That we are all one, these folks and me
And the vote which came, although it sounds daft
Was only myself, reminding myself, about that

Alexandra Dedman

Deal or no Deal?
(Found poem, Gaming Machine,
Wetherspoons, Bristol, 5th March 2019)

Deal or no deal?
Will you go all the way?

Gamble for the chance to upgrade
Super mystery
Diamonds?
Jackpots?
What's in your box?

Deal or no deal?
Free spins
Action spins
Power spins
Every spin's a win!

Deal or no deal?
Win big
Collect mega
Super winnings
Every spin's a win!

Deal or no deal?
Banker spins
Banker bonus
Box of tricks
Every spin's a win!

Deal or no deal?
Will you go all the way?

Play now!

Garry Maguire

The Pitch

A weepie for a troubled time
– think star-crossed lovers, hint of grime.
Since they rubbed out his EMA
Romelu's trying to fill his day
looking for jobs that don't exist
and dossing in the playground, pissed.
It's gaming where he earns respect
and that's how he and Jules connect.
She's up at uni, studying law.
She knows what education's for
but now there's Rom, who's cool and smart;
Assassin's Creed controls her heart.
Eternal love, that's what they wrote
until – ta da! – the Brexit vote.
Rom watches Osborne on the screen;
the smuggest man he's ever seen
says opting out would be naïve.
That does it: Rom is backing LEAVE.
But Jules is voting for REMAIN
disgusted by the Leave campaign –
that whopping slogan on the bus,
the tempting tale of them and us.
We've documentary stuff galore
on feuding families, all-out war.
Make Brexit sexy, give it large;
maybe a cameo for Farage?
Treasure the special thing they had –
the Oxford girl, the Wearside lad -
before their destiny supplied
this all-embracing suicide.
Pull back. Soft focus. Hold it there:
a crane shot of the fateful pair
as Sheeran's vocals fill the air.

Paul Francis

88

The Death of Another Archduke

April looms, and more crueller have come
Yet,
The dead roots don't stir but
Speak evils; nostalgia told
And tended amongst
The sparked – the fiery, beaten
Country; the dead land's lilacs.

The Lady of Situations
Is a cold feed here, no?
All the leads turned cold
On the encapsulated City Unreal.
A younger school now,
Over London Bridge;
Banners, placards, and some
Platitudes, yes. The newest vegetable
Patch denied whatever left of the
The grass.

Of course, we're all economists here.
You! Hypocrite; Calming rhetoric.
This country; yours bound to
Barren bystanders are guiltier than us all.
I was told to get me some teeth. And
As shantih shovels us sense past,
We close the covenants, and at last! They say; the archduke's dead.

Nicky Osborn

We Were Never Truly In

We were never truly in
We'll never be truly out,
This hard or soft Breck's Isle we seek
Is a Round Table roundabout.

A Round Table has no leader,
A lone nation has no place,
"We demand to be Kings of Europe - or else…
We'll disappear without trace!"

Once Breck, King of All Little Britain,
Paid sea-wolves to help him defend
Breck's Island against its invaders
Now those sea-wolves rule without end.

A Round Table has no leader,
A lone nation has no place,
"We demand to be Kings of Europe - or else…
We'll disappear without trace!"

We're the one at the Table insisting
'We stand alone, *merci m'sieu*!'
Safe behind national borders
Hard as nails, though the nails aren't secure.

A Round Table has no leader,
A lone nation has no place,
"We demand to be Kings of Europe - or else
We'll disappear without trace!"

Singing "not from our part of the world, bye "
- To the world inside our Breck's isle,
- To its goods on our continental shelf,
- To its services with a smile.

A Round Table has no leader,
A lone nation has no place,
"We demand to be Kings of Europe - or else…
We'll disappear without trace!"

Gareth Calway

Tommy's 100th

As fossilised as a *Daily Mail* font,
We gather for remembrance, Brexit-badged
With poppies pinned tweet-loud, Union-flagged
Against the Europe we won then didn't want;
The dying leaves in wild gusts blowing blunt
Our inside-out umbrellas like the rags
Of Empire, this annual beret-ing wag's
Self-crowned Napoleon pushing to the Front.

And yet (as MIXED RACE BRITAIN WINS F1
IN GERMAN CAR) for King, Country (and up lines
Dividing Indian, Arab, Jew) the names
Peal off a tongue that joins us all
And ends with… *Captain Lancelot Percival
Williamson*, knights of faith: these countrymen.

Gareth Calway

Slide One *(Presentation Notes)* – **The Sundering of the Kingdom**

What really caused the dissolution of the United Kingdom? The successful second Scottish referendum, with its subsequent annexation of parts of Northern England and the controversial construction of the Hadrian Demilitarized Zone?

Or the infamous parliamentary riots that ultimately turned England into a corporatocracy, ruled over by the one percent barons?

Those events certainly contributed to Wales being carved into survivalist encampments and descent of Northern Ireland into civil war. All agree history would be very different if the United Kingdom had not exited the European Union. But they were just the first dominoes to fall; worse was to follow…

Selina Lock

The Word

Before the coming of the Word, they gather round the fire, the flames dance shadows into life on the walls.
Charcoal grease smears the rockface; crude pictograms conjuring fruitful hunts and full bellies.

Time's hourglass sands run on, and the Word takes root. Nations sit in council chambers.
They debate and negotiate, celebrating their differences, but sharing common purpose to achieve the same ends.

The Word promises much and often delivers more: prosperity, community, illumination.
The Word is a seed, planted in open minds, fertilised with good intentions. Dry soil turned fertile; it blooms.

The Word builds bridges, not walls.

Jay Eales

We don't talk about Brexit anymore

My parents voted for brexit.
I still don't really know why,
since we are among the people
the extremists want to die …
… or go back to their own countries;
whatever it is they say.
'immigrants drain this country'
and the English are the who ones who pay.
But I've had a job since I was thirteen
Contributed since then too.
I pay all of my taxes
Don't like it but I do.
Something got to my parents
To make them vote for *this*
I blame the town we moved to
When my sister and I were just kids.
It's in towns like ours they brainwash you -
They claim there aren't enough jobs
Always demonizing the 'other'
Spouting rubbish from far right gods.
I guess that's how they got to *my* parents
Both black british born and bred
Mum and dad voting leave
'Remain' my sister and I said.
Brexit has split this country
and it split my family too -
My parents are no longer together
Ironic what brexit can do.

Ayodele

Brexile

My favourite uncle's immigrant quip,
dear old Grandma's darky joke,
next door neighbour's UKIP sign…

My country's tired of folk like me,
isn't interested in what we say.
You see, now it's taken back control,

it thinks it's Dunkirk all over again.
Either we should dig in and stay. Or leave.
Either way, a part of me's already gone.

Craig Dobson

Farewell from Dublin

There's smugness in the air
And a haughty look on people's faces;
Because they shot themselves in the foot -
They let themselves be cheated.

The men with big mouths;
Tricksy words spilled from their lips.
That filled their heads with big notions and
Left their country in shit!

My Granny used to drive
The three hours to the border,
Used to open the boot and
Let them rifle through her motor.

On the 24th of June,
Her wet cheeks watched the telly.
Her eyes saw the guns
Outside the schools and maybe -

They wanted a change
To stick it to the suits;
A new day for their children
To scream tongues that felt mute

They forget there's a world
On the other side of the channel,
They've never seen the barbed walls -
They've never heard of Omagh.

When the far away buildings
Have left the streets full of sickness;
If they can't choose to be European
Why the fuck would they be British?

Richard Kilian Neville

Thank God for British Values

Let's take back our borders,
take back our jobs, take back our wives -
we're suspicious, we're frightened,
we can't see their eyes.

We're alarmed, we're threatened,
by their work ethic and willing,
May's strong and stable mantra–
with their presence, they are killing.

We're entitled, we're ready:
let's make Britain ~~great~~ white
with our Anglo-Saxon, Viking, Roman blood,
we're ready to fight.

Although we are all mongrels,
God save the Queen
for she understands what British values mean –
we cry BREXIT MEANS BREXIT in the working man's clubs
and toast to the future
of our independent 'no deal'
we cry, LET'S TAKE BACK OUR BORDERS
for we heard it on TV
and we trust in news for our ideas to form.

Isabelle Kenyon

Breaking Point

It all started on Twitter after
someone said something
about the *Untied* Kingdom.

Some called it   unacceptable,
some called it   a typo,
and some called   family.
Terror and rage built within days.
Shared   thousands of times.
#Untied,   what do you mean,
UNTIED?   People argued.
People argued,   loud and proud,
'We need to fight for our country,
for what's left   of our country!'
'What about   those left behind?'
So that's how   what can't happen
keeps happening.   Am I
reading this?   Are we
really   screaming this?
#Untied, #untied,   their Kingdom
for a side.   And it went:
Liberated!   Isolated!
Soul costing!   Cost saving!
Sovereign!   Selfish!
Xenophobic!   Safe!
Democratic!   Fascist!
Egalitarian!   Unfair!
Finally as rich   as we deserve.
It's not   our fault
some don't   deserve it.
And free!   Yes, free!
State!   Movement!
All we   want,
all   anyone
ever   wants,
is   to
be   free.

They   won.

'It's not	a war',
they said,	but
they	won.
52	48
I meet	them
every	day.
Ireland	awaits.
Scotland	hopes.
We all	tremble.
How lonely	it feels,
being	United.

Lou Sarabadzic

Red Boots

I.

My mother, pre-teen and pakistani and too pure for swear words,
Shouted RED SHOES! at the red-shoed mean girl
In her moment of courage against the oppressor.
The ultimate insult she could think to hurl.
Her daughter, half ode, half rebellion, bought a pair of red boots
With her first wad of dog-walker wages.
But daughter.
Why this need for stomping and stamping
And littering your footprints like exclamation marks?
But mother.
How else will I find my way home?

II.

These boots are worn from years of not treading softly.
The sole is flayed thin,
The skin cracked.
I'm not ready to say they're a lost cause-
I want to scrub them down and paint them anew.
My younger sister votes floral or paisley,
My mother votes for the bin or plain black,
And I want uncomfortable words.

III.

The poem I'll write all over my boots
Needs to be almost unreadable.
Whether or not about the darkness of night
Or the impertinence of newborn bloom,
The lines will split between two kicks
So if you insist on borders and barriers between,
You'll not recognise them as poetry.

Mariya Pervez

Settled

31 years with ILR. 3 months with SS.
I registered, to make me feel safe.
Did I make the world unsafe
for those who cannot register?

Noornorth

ILR stands for "Indefinite Leave to Remain", and SS, "Settled Status".

Thought for the Day

It's a quarter to eight. We are thankful,
or not, for divine interventions
from imams, rabbis, priests and theologians.
They deliver us from drizzle and Brexit.

Even thugs and sceptics can find light
in the musings of a vicar
who doesn't mention Gods but speaks of hope
in shared humanity, omits

allusions to any notions of morality.
She has no big questions for listeners today;
a small one works for all of us:
will we be okay?

Mark Connors

Roundabout turns

While Soviet smiles
Don Trump yawns
        Chasms and higher walls to build
          Photographs of ghettoes
                Adorn the walls of power
      While boats drift on currency
Ticktock, stocks, tock tick rocks, flocks
                Blood on the wires
         Death camps waiting
         UKIP Jackboots, genocide
                Roundabout turns
            Vote to stay, one world
            No state labels of hate
No more Omarska, Ramasko
No more Srebrenica, Nicbarense
No more Birkenau, Ubirekan
No more Mezireh, Herizem
          Pray that the tears wash away their pain, but not the
      memories
          We can be together again…

Tim Bombdog

A Psalm of Donald

1 Bigotry is my shepherd; Huddled masses shall not pass. **2** I maketh them to cower down in tender age cages. Or bleedeth beside storm waters. **3** I promoteth our nepotism. I leadeth you in the paths of racist-ness for profits name's sake. **4** Yea, though I tweet through the valley of the shadow of threat; I will fear no facts; for my genius is with me; my dog whistles and misogyny, they comfort me. **5** I preparest a wall before me in the face of fake enemies: I anointest my bouffant with lacquer; my gob runneth over. **6** Surely, spray tan and pussy shall follow me all the days of my term; and I will pimp from the shit house of narcissism, forever and ever...

A Man.

Trevor Wright

The Remainer's Prayer

In the name of Brexit
Deliver us not
unto Trumpism

Ambrose Musiyiwa

CONTRIBUTORS

Alexandra Dedman was born and raised in County Durham and has recently moved back. She is proud mum to one lovely son. She also works as a Freelance Science Writer and does a bit of poetry on the side.

Ambrose Musiyiwa edited *Leicester 2084 AD: New Poems about the City* (CivicLeicester, 2018) and co-edited *Welcome to Leicester* (Dahlia Publishing, 2016). He is the author of *The Gospel According to Bobba*. His poems and short stories have been featured in several anthologies.

Andy Callen and **Wayne McDonald** are the main songwriters for Manchester-based alternative country band, Picnic Area. Their most recent album "No country for young men" was heavily influenced by Brexit and other world events.

Angi Holden is a writer and Creative Writing lecturer, whose published work includes poetry, short stories and flash fictions. Her story *Painting Stones for Virginia* was a runner-up in the 2018 Cheshire Prize for Literature. Her poetry pamphlet *Spools of Thread*, won the inaugural Mothers Milk Books Pamphlet Prize.

Anne Howkins has been writing fiction for about ten years, after taking the OU Creative Writing course. She is an active member of Fosseway Writer's Group. Anne is a recent convert to flash fiction and has had short stories published in magazines and anthologies. She has been campaigning for a People's Vote.

Antonia Langford is an eighteen-year-old aspiring poet from Manchester. She trains with the spoken word collective Young Identity, has had her poems published in several small journals, performs regularly at open mics and was recently commissioned to write a poem for the Greater Manchester Green Summit.

Leicester-born political activist **Anthony L Church** is a founder member of Loughborough-based Stage Left Theatre Workshop. Scripts he has written include *A Man of Humble Beginnings*, *Bella and the Tyger-Man*, and an adaptation of *Hansel and Gretel*. He has also had several short stories and poems published.

Bethany Rivers has two collections: *the sea refuses no river*, from Fly on the Wall Press and *Off the wall*, from Indigo Dreams. She is the author of *Fountain of Creativity: Ways to nourish your writing*, from Victorina Press. She teaches and mentors the writing of poetry and stories: www.writingyourvoice.org.uk

Carole Coates has had four collections published by Shoestring Press (the latest of which is *Jacob*, 2016) which will publish her pamphlet *The Stories They Told Her* in May. Wayleave Press published her pamphlet *Crazy Days* in 2014. In 2017 she won the second prize in the Mslexia Poetry Competition.

Ceinwen E Cariad Haydon lives in Newcastle upon Tyne, UK, and writes short stories and poetry. She has been widely published in web magazines and in print anthologies. She graduated with an MA in Creative Writing from Newcastle University in 2017. She believes everyone's voice counts.

Charis Cooper is a German born singer-songwriter, actor, and poet. She's made her home in the UK, near Brighton, where she lives with her two daughters and her hyperactive imagination.

Chloë Jacquet is a multi-slam winning, multicultural, multifaceted spoken word artist based in Gloucestershire. Her work deals with a wide variety of subjects, ranging from workplace discrimination and mental health, to the pressures placed on modern men, via her short term relationship with a biscuit. Chloë can be found on social media @ChloeJPoetry

Colin Gardiner lives and works in Coventry UK. He writes short stories and poetry. He is currently studying a Masters degree in Creative Writing at the University of Leicester.

Dr Corinne Fowler is an Associate Professor at the University of Leicester and author of *Postcolonial Manchester* and *Green Unpleasant Land: Creative Responses to Rural Britain's Colonial Connections* (forthcoming, Peepal Tree Press, 2020). She leads a child-led history and writing project called "Colonial Countryside: National Trust Houses Reinterpreted".

Craig Dobson has had poems published in various poetry magazines in Britain and Europe. He works as a university librarian in London, where he has met many European colleagues who have all brought a great deal to this country. He's fifty and, since Brexit, has never felt so ashamed of being British.

Danielle Allen is a writer from Newcastle upon Tyne. Her short horror fiction has been published in several print anthologies, and she has been shortlisted in many writing competitions. She has been screenwriting for the last two years. Danielle is a remoaner and proud leftie snowflake.

David R Mellor is from Liverpool, England. He spent his late teen homeless in Merseyside. He found understanding and belief through words, and his work has been aired widely, at the BBC, The Tate, galleries and pubs and everything in between.

Deborah Harvey is a Bristol poet and novelist. Her poems have been widely published in journals and anthologies, and broadcast on Radio 4's *Poetry Please*. Her fourth poetry collection, *The Shadow Factory*, will be published by Indigo Dreams in summer 2019. Deborah is co-director of The Leaping Word poetry consultancy.

Deborah Tyler-Bennett is a poet, and fiction writer with eight volumes of poems, and three of short linked stories to her credit. Her new volume, *Ken Dodd Takes a Holiday*, will be out from King's England in 2019, and she's currently working on her first novel, *Livin' in a Great Big Way*. She's always valued being a citizen of Europe.

Elizabeth Uter has taught poetry workshops for Farrago Poetry and Kensington & Chelsea Library Services. In May 2018, she won the Poem for Slough Competition in two categories: 19's and over and was the overall winner with her poem 'Slough Homecoming' an antidote to Sir John Betjeman's scathing poem, 'Slough'.

Ellie Curtis graduated from the University of York with an English degree in 2015, and recently completed an MA in Gender Studies at University College Dublin. She currently lives in North London and teaches English to children with special educational needs.

Emma Baines has published poetry in magazines and journals including *The Lampeter Review*, *Roundyhouse*, *Cambria* and *POEM*. In 2011, she edited and contributed to 'The Month had 32 Days', published by Parthian. She has read at festivals and events, translated work from Welsh for Menna Elfyn and her own writing has been included in installation by glass artist Linda Norris.

Gareth Calway is a published poet, novelist, playwright, lyricist and member of folkband, the Penland Phezants. His works include *Doin Different* (Poppyland, 2016) and *Bound for Jamaica* (Collins, 2012.) Like Eric Idle and John Major, he resented his birthday (March 29) being stolen for Brexit Day 2019. These poems are his revenge. https://youtu.be/yZnhn_I6hXk

Garry Maguire is a writer who one day went to a place so imbued with the spirit of Brexit that even the gaming machine seemed to scream propaganda.
\
Glen Wilson lives in Portadown. He has been widely published having work in *The Honest Ulsterman, Iota, The Interpreter's House* amongst others. He won the Seamus Heaney Award for New Writing 2017 and the Jonathan Swift Creative Writing Award in 2018. His first collection of poetry is coming out in 2019 with Doire Press.

Harry Gallagher is widely published, runs the north east stanza of the Poetry Society and is continually appalled at what has happened to the people of his class, in his area of his country. When enraged he falls into hapless rhyme, for which he apologises.

Isabella Mead works as a storytelling teacher and trainer in literary museums. Her poetry has appeared in *Magma*, *Poetry News* and *Envoi*. She has been Highly Commended in the Bridport Prize (2016), Longlisted in the National Poetry Competition (2018), and commended in the Cafe Writers Prize (2019).

Isabelle Kenyon is northern poet and the author of *Digging Holes To Another Continent* (Clare Songbirds Publishing House). She is the editor of Fly on the Wall Press. Her poems have been published in poetry anthologies by Indigo Dreams Publishing, Verve Poetry Press, and Hedgehog Poetry Press. Her book reviews, articles and blog posts have been published in various places such as Neon Books, Authors Publish, Harness magazine and Five Oaks Press.
www.isabellekenyonpoetry.wordpress.com

Jacob Lund's poetry has been published in *Openings*, the annual anthology of The Open University and in *N2 Poetry*, London. He has worked as a reviewer for the *Daily Telegraph*, and has published on Shakespeare in academic journals. He lives in Brighton.

Jacob Spivey is a writer at the University of Leicester. He writes poetry, screenplay, short stories and whatever else he is inspired to create. When he's not writing he's watching movies, supporting his football team or studying hard.

Jay Eales was born among the dying embers of the Swinging Sixties in the East Midlands. He switches hats as writer, editor, publisher, journalist and teacher, and produced the *Do Something* zine as a response to the Brexit referendum through Factor Fiction. www.factorfictionpress.co.uk

Joe Williams is a writer and performing poet from Leeds. In 2017 his debut pamphlet, *Killing the Piano*, was published by Half Moon Books, and he won the Open Mic Competition at Ilkley Literature Festival. His second book, the verse novella *An Otley Run*, was shortlisted in the 2019 Saboteur Awards www.joewilliams.co.uk

Joel Baccas is a regular contributor to InFacts, Brexitshambles and is part of the MyCitizenship.EU team.

John Merrell began poetry thinking in 2004 when his redeployment meant a longer commute which allowed words and their rhythms to materialise. He has written many poems particularly since he retired in 2012 as well as attempting play-writing because he enjoys the fractured interaction between dialogue and meaning.

Julian Stannard teaches at the University of Winchester. He taught at the University of Genoa for many years and his latest book of poetry is *Sottoripa* (Canneto Publishers, 2018), a bilingual publication of his Italian writing. He reviews for *TLS*.

Katherine Cleave is a Fine Artist living in Barnes. Since graduating from Goldsmiths College, her artwork has been displayed at several London galleries and events, presenting an ironic play of words, phrases and images juxtaposed to create a lively stage on which to probe reality. Recent work includes a small collection of poems.

Kathy Zwick taught History and English in an international school in London for over 20 years. Many of her poems recycle themes from old lesson plans. She has had poems published in several UK anthologies, among them, Hippocrates Prize2010, Brownsbank Anthology, Hand Luggage Only, In Protest, VER2015, and Wolverhampton Literary Festival2018.

Kelly Knight (31) is a British writer, poet and teacher of English Language and Literature, currently living in Barcelona. More of her work can be found via Instagram @own_two_feet

Lizza Lane is an amateur poet, based in the North West of England. Her work normally focuses on politics, identity, the mountains and the seaside. She enjoys 90s indie music, playing with her cat Jed, and adventuring in the Lake District.

Lou Sarabadzic is a French bilingual poet, blogger, and novelist living in the UK. She has published two books in French: a novel, *La Vie verticale*, and a poetry collection, *Ensemble*. In January 2018, she received the Dot Award for Digital Literature for the #NERDSproject: nerdsproject.com. Follow her on Twitter @lousarabadzic.

Mantz Yorke lives in Manchester. His poems have appeared in a number of print magazines, anthologies and e-magazines in the UK, Ireland, Israel, Canada, the US, Australia and Hong Kong.

Mark Connors is an award winning poet and novelist from Leeds, widely published in the UK and overseas. His debut pamphlet *Life is a Long Song* was published by OWF Press in 2015. His debut collection *Nothing is Meant to be Broken* was published by Stairwell Books in 2017. For more info visit www.markconnors.co.uk

Mark Rutter's poems have appeared in many magazines and anthologies, and his most recent pamphlet is *Basho in Acadia* (Flarestack). He is also a painter and book-artist, and his most recent artist's book is *Homage to Andrei Tarkovsky* (Tatlin Books). A collection of minimal poems is due from inkConcrete next year, and he is currently working on a series of collaborative monoprints with Kate Dicker.

Mariya Pervez is in the third person.

Melissa Oram is currently in her third year reading for a BA in History at the University of Exeter. She is a dual national and an enthusiastic pro-EU supporter, having backed Exeter Students For Europe's campaign over the last few months, and published her poem "March" on their blog. Melissa has recently also set up her own poetry blog, and is the current Vice President for Exeter University's Creative Writing Society.

Michael Woods is a poet and lecturer in English Literature. He has three collections published by Templar Poetry: *Absence Notes* (2011); *Algebra* (2017) and *Opening Time* (2018): http://michaeljwoods.me.uk

Michele Witthaus has been a professional journalist, copywriter and editor for more than 30 years. Several of her poems have been published in various media and she also reads at events in Leicester and elsewhere. Michele is a member of the Leicester Writers' Club.

Molly Burns is a poet and Creative Writing PhD student. She lives by the sea and can often be found ranting about the benefits of pebble beaches versus sand or tweeting about the cats she meets day to day. If you would like to know more, follow her on Twitter at @TheMollBurns, or see more work at themollyburns.com.

Nathan Evans is a writer, director and performer whose work has been funded by Arts Council England, toured by the British Council, archived by the British Film Institute and broadcast on Channel 4 television. His poetry has been published by Dead Ink, Inky Needles, Poetry Space and Manchester Metropolitan University. His first collection, Threads, is published by Inkandescent, his second, CNUT is launched in November www.nathanevans.co.uk

Neil Fulwood has published two collections with Shoestring Press and two pamphlets with the Black Light Engine Room Press. He co-edited the Alan Sillitoe tribute anthology, *More Raw Material*, with David Sillitoe. His poetry, reviews and short fiction have been widely published in print and online journals. He lives and works in Nottingham.

Nick Browne is an established novelist and an almost novice poet.

Nicky Osborn is a 23-year old poet living in London. Strongly influenced by T.S. Eliot, he aims to use succinct tones reminiscent of 'The Waste Land' to draw comparisons between the prevailing sterility and potential economic disaster.

Nicollen Meek is a reformed PR professional from London. She is currently working on her first collection of poems.

Nusrat M Haider is a personal advisor in Leicester City Council. She has been working in Social Care and Health for 14 years. Nusrat likes reading sci fi, history novels and poetry.

Pam Thompson is a poet and educator based in Leicester. Her publications include *The Japan Quiz* (Redbeck Press, 2009) and *Show Date and Time*, (Smith | Doorstop, 2006). Pam's second collection, *Strange Fashion*, was published by Pindrop Press in 2017. She is a 2019 Hawthornden Fellow.

Pappageno is a fifty-something classical opera fan and enthusiastic traveler with a thirst for new cultures. He despairs at today's tacky, so-called 'celebrity' culture and the dumbing down of society. A passionate anti-Brexit European, Pappageno hardly ever writes poetry.

Paul Francis is a prolific, versatile poet, living in Much Wenlock. He has published two collections and a range of topical pamphlets, and is active in local readings. He has been placed in six national poetry competitions, and *Sonnets with notes* will be published later this year.

Philip Burton has been labourer, traveller, professional student, amateur actor, Lancashire headteacher, poetry practitioner for children (as Pip The Poet), and lately a multi-award-winning poet. His recent poems, titled *His Usual Theft*, was published in 2017 by Indigo Dreams Press.

PR Walker recently returned to writing poetry after a gap of thirty years. One aspect of his new body of work is an exploration of the "the state we're in". Previously one of his poems won a competition, a new poem has just been "specially commended" in a recent Irish competition.

Rachel Hardisty Vincent is an aspiring poet currently completing an Open University course in Creative Writing. She lives in Cambridgeshire with her ever-supportive husband Russell.

Richard Kilian Neville is a 21 year old 3rd year European Studies student at Trinity College, Dublin who lives in Cabinteely, Ireland. Currently unpublished, Richard enjoys writing about themes including politics, mental health, adolescence and sexuality.

Rob Lowe lives in North Wales, in a tiny flat too full of books for comfort. He does not own a television, any games consoles; a washing machine, freezer or microwave; car or motorcycle; or have central heating. He is a member of Colwyn Bay Writers' Circle.

Sam Smith is editor of **The Journal** magazine and publisher of **Original Plus** books. Author of several novels and collections of poetry, he presently lives in Blaengarw, South Wales https://sites.google.com/site/samsmiththejournal/

Sarra Culleno is a teacher and mother, writing and performing both formal and free verse poetry. Sarra performs at poetry open mics and slams acoss the Uk, and was longlisted for the Cinnamon Press Pamphlet Prize 2019. She is appearing as a featured poet at Herstories Festival. Sarra is on YouTube and Spoken Label https://spokenlabel.bandcamp.com/

Sean McDonagh is a poet from Birmingham, living in London and working in publishing to promote interdisciplinary and intersectional writing. He has had poetry published in *Allegro*, *Rockland* and *Foxtrot Uniform*.

Selina Lock is a mild-mannered librarian from Leicester. In her alternative life in comics she edited *The Girly Comic*, is a writing tutor and has written strips for various comic strip anthologies, including the double-Eisner nominated *To End All Wars*. She has had several short stories and a novella published.

Stephen Regan's poems have been published in *Envoi, Reach Poetry, Killing the Angel, Dove Tales*, *The Quality of Mersey* anthology and *Fragile Things* anthology. For 12 years Stephen also wrote as "Sam Brady: The Man They Can't Gag" for *ITV's Oracle* and *Teletext* services. @StephenJRegan https://stephenreganwriter.com/

Stephen Wylie was born in Glasgow a long time ago, but his early life was spent mostly in Ayrshire. Upon graduating from Glasgow University, he moved to Leicester, and has been here ever since. He took up writing late in life, and has had poetry previously published in four local anthologies.

Steve Pottinger is a born story-teller. His latest collection *a fine fine place* followed on from the acclaimed *more bees, bigger bonnets*. He has entertained audiences the length and breadth of the UK, and is also a member of the Poets, Prattlers, and Pandemonialists collective in Wolverhampton.

Trefor Stockwell studied English at Bangor University, and has recently completed his PhD in Creative Writing. He now lives on the Isle of Anglesey where he concentrates on writing and performing poetry, and is currently working on a picaresque novel with the working title of 'The Lost'.

Tim Bombdog is Leicester's very own post-punk poet combining hard-hitting revolutionary poetry, with wit, humour, and a touch of sensitivity. He has performed to widespread acclaim at venues around the UK and has worked closely with his friend Jean Binta Breeze MBE in developing his portfolio of work.

Tim Cumming's collections include *The Miniature Estate* (1991), *Apocalypso* (1992, 1999), *Contact Print* (2002), *The Rumour* (2004), *The Rapture* (2011) *Etruscan Miniatures* (2012) and *Rebel Angels in the Mind Shop* (2015). *Knuckle,* is due this July. His work has appeared in The Forward's *Poems of the Decade*, the WS Graham anthology, *The Caught Habits of Language* and Bloodaxe's *Identity Parade*.

Tracy Davidson lives in Warwickshire, England, and writes poetry and flash fiction. Her work has appeared in various publications and anthologies, including: *Poet's Market*, *Mslexia*, *AtlasPoetica*, *Writing Magazine*, *Modern Haiku*, *The Binnacle*, *A Hundred Gourds*, *Shooter*, *Journey to Crone*, *The Great Gatsby Anthology*, *WAR* and *In Protest: 150 Poems for Human Rights*.

Trevor Wright works part time in social care specialising in autism. His second collection, *Salt Flow*, was published by Big White Shed in April 2019 and he is currently Shadow Writer to Rob Gee at Glenfield Hospital on the Elder Tree Project.

Trinity-Grace Robinson was born in 2002 and has been writing since she was a child. Currently a student, she will leave school in 2019 and is passionate about writing poetry and short stories. She is hoping to be a poet and is working hard to get her work seen by the community.

Yvonne Reddick is the author of *Translating Mountains* (Seren, 2017), which won the Mslexia pamphlet prize. Her poetry pamphlet *Spikenard* (2019) is a Laureate's Choice. An associate editor at Magma magazine, she has won awards from New Writing North, Creative Futures and the Poetry Society. She lectures in Creative Writing.

ACKNOWLEDGMENTS

'A Song for Europe' by Joe Williams was originally published on the Algebra of Owls webzine in 2016

'Bad bad man' and 'Where I'm from' by Andy Callen and 'No country for young men' by Wayne McDonald are lyrics from Picnic Area's third studio album "No country for young men"

'Beyond this …' by Stephen Regan has been published by the e-zine *Poetry24*

An earlier version of '"Bollocks" and Its Uses: a Short History' by Joel Baccas was first published by Madeleina Kay on Bollockstobrexit.com

'March' by Melissa Oram has also been published on Exeter Students for Europe's blog

'Measures' has been published in *Opening Time* by Michael Woods (Templar Poetry, 2018, p.42)

'Peregines' by Yvonne Reddick was first published in *Midnight Listening: The Jerwood/Arvon Mentoring Programme* anthology 2018

'Thank God for British Values', by Isabelle Kenyon, has previously has been previously published in *Persona Non Grata* by Fly on the Wall Press

'The game was won', by Trinity-Grace Robinson, was published in the 2018 Between These Shores Literary and Arts Annual

'When the world fell in on Birstall' was published in *Nothing is meant to be Broken* by Mark Connors (Stairwell Books, 2017)

22587548R00083

Printed in Great Britain
by Amazon